Margaret

From

Gerrie

Date

2010 - 11 - 29

www.carpediem.co.za

A Small Book of Joy
published by Carpe Diem Media

First edition, first print 2007
ISBN 978-1-920156-94-7

Typesetting • Zelda Botha
Editor and Translator • Marié Henning
Cover design • Magdie Claasens
Photos • The Bigger Picture/Photo-objects (PO)
Printed and bound by Creda Communications

CONTACT DETAILS
Carpe Diem Media
PO Box 5801 Vanderbijlpark 1900
Tel • (016) 982 3617 Fax • (016) 982 3618
E-mail • boeke@carpediem.co.za

Nina Smit

a small book of Joy

carpe diem MEDIA

Joy

The secret to happiness

The secret to real happiness lies in discovering the insignificant, trivial things that are part of life – the things that are taken for granted too often. Look at these things and treasure them – make a deliberate effort to enjoy them every day so that your life can be filled with joy.

Create happiness

It is assumed that personal happiness comes from being creative. Creative people are happy because it fills your life with joy when you create things. The more creative you are, the happier you will become ... Busy people don't have time to fret. So, get creative and guarantee your own happiness!

Be a creator of joy

After you have completed a task well you are most likely finely attuned to the things that make you happy. Then you are able to take a step back from your own life and see other people ... this will remind you of a hundred things that have the ability to make you happy.

Plant a seed of joy

By doing certain things – and refraining from doing others – you can become a creator of joy who not only ensures your own happiness, but also plants a seed of joy in other people. Make an effort to look for things that make you happy, and share them with others.

Enjoy life

You are allowed to find pleasure in worldly and trivial things ... things like the crispy crust of freshly-baked bread, the first golden daffodils of the season, or the sound of rain against the windowpane ... Fill your heart with beauty so that your life can be fruitful and valuable.

Beauty makes you happy

Most of us are always in such a hurry that the beauty of life passes us by. Still, nobody can deny that beauty makes you happy. People who haven't learned to see, appreciate and treasure the beauty around them yet, miss out on so much.

Treasure your memories

Discover the delights hidden in the smallest of things: the excessive yellow of a sunflower, or the soft pink and violet hues of the sweat-peas in the back garden ... Start cherishing these fine memories for the days when there may not be anything beautiful left to see.

Smile!

Pull up the corners of your mouth, smile and be happy! Smile at everyone who crosses your path because a smile is free of charge, but it has the ability to do so much. It enriches the life of the one receiving it without taking anything away from the one giving it. Take special care to make your smile an inherent part of your life so that it will come naturally.

Be cheerful!

Decide what it means to have a cheerful disposition and determine its characteristics. If you want to be happy, you have to help others be happy. If you serve others selflessly you will find nobility, satisfaction and joy deep within your soul.

Learn to laugh again

In order to experience true happiness, you have to learn to laugh again. Surround yourself with people who know how to laugh and who have mastered the art of enjoying life. Let them wet your curiosity about their amusing lifestyle and let them teach you how to laugh again!

The lessons of suffering

If hardship and suffering come knocking at life's door, remember that they cross your path to bring you even closer to your Creator. Experiencing hardship is always a good thing, even if it's not very nice. See hardship as a blessing, because it helps you grow ...

Hope in happiness

When things are really bad, just remind yourself that your future still lies ahead. That makes life worthwhile. Also remember that you are entitled to a new vision for a happy and purposeful life. Then you will be able to keep on hoping and being happy, even in times of crisis.

Life is precious!

It is a fact of life that people who have experienced hardship can enjoy happiness with much more intensity and gratitude than those who have had it easy all their life. Only when you have been at death's door do you realise how wonderful it is to be healthy and how precious life really is!

Relax and enjoy!

If, perhaps, you are one of those perfectionists who set yourself goals that are impossible to achieve – don't you want to choose today not to do that any more? Why don't you rather relax a bit, sit in the sun, rediscover the joys of life, and enjoy the life you have been given.

Overflowing love

Love always generates happiness. God wants His love to be fountains that well up inside you and flow over to the people you come into contact with. Then you will experience happiness in your life – a happiness rooted in His love for you.

Seeing happiness

If the dark clouds of adversity build up on your life's horizon, put on your glasses and see the rainbow through the clouds. And even if the clouds are very dense, remember that the sun still shines brightly beyond them!

Happiness is … now!

We often dream of the nice things we are going to do … someday. In the process we let the joys of the present slip us by. We forget to listen to our children when they are still young, until later – when they are grown up – and they don't want to talk to us any more. Don't let the joys on offer today slip you by just because you want to save them for later!

The secret to happiness

The secret to happiness is seeing the joys of the present and cherishing them in your heart, to live life to the full ... today! It is being able to recognise and enjoy the present moment and making a list of all the undeserved blessings you receive every day!

Enjoy every moment

Warm yourself in the warmth of today's joys, and don't let one more day pass you by or be wasted without squeezing every bit of joy from it that you can. Rejoice in today. Do whatever comes to hand, and make a concerted effort to enjoy everything nice that is on offer today!

A sense of humour makes life easier

If you have a good sense of humour, happiness will never be far from you. A sense of humour helps you deal with hardship and to accept your failures. Therefore, practise having a sense of humour, and develop it by noticing the amusing things around you and sharing them with other people.

Laugh at yourself

Most of us take life way too serious. Maybe we should learn to laugh at ourselves, and to not be ashamed of admitting our own mistakes. Once you can laugh at your own mistakes, you will probably discover that you are not as ashamed of them any more.

Happiness is contagious

You have to know a secret to experience true happiness: When you make other people happy, that joy will spread to your own life. You can't see the happiness in someone else's eyes without having it ignite a spark of happiness in your own heart.

Make others happy

Happiness doesn't have to be something extraordinary. Doing something for a good cause, performing an essential service or doing something simple to help another person can make you happy.

Give with love

Is giving a blessing or a burden to you? You shouldn't only give of yourself to other people; you should also give some of your means. But always keep in mind that the way you give is just as important as what your give. Whether you are giving of yourself or your means – it depends on the attitude with which you give.

Happiness in words

I can't help thinking of books when I think of words. And there are precious few things that make me as happy as my books! If something precious is said in a new and original way, it makes me want to shriek with joy. It gets better every time I read it. Each book eventually becomes a personal friend that provides me with endless pleasure.

Forgotten pleasures

It is nice to take a brand-new book off the shelf and smell its newness, but it is just as nice to buy an old favourite at a street market for next to nothing. Be that as it may – why don't you make time to read something pleasant again and enjoy the forgotten pleasures it offers?

Don't look past happiness

People often look for happiness by accumulating wealth, stocking up on "security" for the day of tomorrow, or gathering their friends around them. Others tend to look for happiness in far away places. By doing this, they miss out on the happiness that is right under their noses ...

The joy of living

People don't always enjoy the pleasant things that happen to them, but they long for these experiences when it is too late. Be certain that you don't let this wonderful life pass you by. Enjoy the present, this moment, and hold every pleasant and beautiful thing offered to you by life today close to your heart.

Happiness is not selfish

We are all selfish by nature. It is impossible for us to love others with an all-encompassing love without asking for anything in return. Happiness means putting an end to selfishness, and learning to put others' needs above your own.

A smile of happiness

You are happy when you smile, rather than smiling because you are happy, writes William James. Therefore, get rid of the frown on your face caused by worry, and decide to share your smile liberally with every person you meet from now on.

Share your smile

You can touch other people's lives by making it a habit to always have a smile on your face. Smile at every grim-faced person you meet; make a concerted effort not only to be friendly with other people, but also to talk to them in a friendly manner.

Your smile will come back

If you can manage to keep on smiling even if things are not going your way, you will find that you feel better afterwards. It is impossible to stay depressed if you smile because, according to an Indian saying, the smile you send out always returns to your own heart.

Become a woman of joy

Is your happiness meter in the red at the moment? You should pause for a while and count all the things that make you happy. Then make a choice to become a woman of joy … a woman who goes looking for happiness no matter what the circumstances are or how negative things may be.

Enjoy with your senses

Rejoice in the ordinary, everyday things you can enjoy with your senses: the sound of rain against the windowpane, a child's shriek of laughter, the words of an exceptional poem, the perfect harmony of a harp concerto, the sound of leaves blowing in the wind, a baby's soft cheek against your own, sunshine and clouds.

A smile is contagious

Friendly people often find that others react to them with friendliness. There are few things that are as contagious as a beaming smile. Try to greet every stranger you meet with a smile. Some of them will look at you with surprise, but most of them will return the smile.

Laughter is medicine

Laughter is medicine – and it's free of charge. Scientists recently discovered that when you laugh your body releases special hormones that help fight stress and depression. In addition, you don't have to pay for it or submit a claim to your medical aid. Start laughing again and feel the stress leave your body.

Be a joyous person

It is possible to be a joyous person every day. Rediscover the joy of knowing for certain Who you belong to. This knowledge will make your joy even greater. Loving the Creator of joy will help you be a woman of joy.

A smile is free

A smile is free, but it can accomplish so much. If you are not a jolly person by nature, you can teach yourself to see the amusing things around you and so start laughing more. You can even try reading humorous books, listening to funny jokes or children's sayings to help you laugh out loud and to relax.

What does your face say?

What do people see when they look at your face? A depressed person with a hunched back and a frowning forehead, or a beaming person with laughter lines at the corners of their eyes? Remember, your facial expression is often a telltale sign for other people to know who you really are and what is going on in your heart.

Firewood for tomorrow

Of all the things that make one happy, cherished memories are the most important. The happy memories of today will be the firewood that protects you against the cold that may be awaiting you tomorrow. So start writing down all your treasured memories today, and revel in them when times are hard.

Be a collector of happiness

Everyone can be a collector of happiness. Furnish a room or corner of your house with things that make you happy – a place where you can sit and read, take a nap or just daydream. See to it that the space is equipped with all the things that brings you joy ... such as a big bouquet of flowers, your favourite books and the soft sounds of your best-loved music.

Share your joy

Cheerless, hopeless people have a way of infecting other people. Luckily, the contrary is also true: optimism is just as contagious. But you shouldn't keep happy days and joyous words to yourself – start today to share your hope and joy with the people around you.

Inextinguishable spark!

If you are a happy person, you can't keep the joy you feel within you inside – as a matter of fact, it just wants to escape. This unquenchable joy is a spark that can ignite the whole world. The more joy you have within you, the easier you will be able to ignite the sparks of joy in other people so that they, too, can light up the world.

Serving with love

In a marriage the partners should serve each other with love. These acts of love are contagious: If your partner sees that you are willing to serve him, he will be willing to serve you. Sooner or later your partner will try and help you or make you happy of his own accord. Then you can serve each other in love and happiness!

Loving care brings joy

You shouldn't only show the people in the inner circle of your family that you love and care for them; this love and care should also be shared with the world outside. Then the people close to you and others can all experience the joy of caring love.

The joy of hospitality

Start to visit with people, and show the people visiting you real, old-fashioned hospitality. Make them feel special and welcome by placing some flowers in their room, putting a nice soap in the bathroom or handing them a note telling them that they are welcome!

Invest in quality

Invest in the quality of your marriage – that is the single most important investment you will ever make! Work with your partner to make your marriage a feast, and keep investing in your marriage so that it will be a treasure chest filled with the things you enjoy about the union.

Joy

Be content

Be content with what you have and who you are. Develop your own unique talents without always comparing yourself to the (in your eyes!) more spectacular talents of others; make the most of your good qualities without blinding yourself to the beauty of others. This will make you a much happier person.

Make use of every opportunity

Put your arm on the shoulder of the person you are talking to, and hug or shake the hand of an acquaintance if you bump into them. Use every opportunity to touch the heart and life of the people you come into contact with, and make them realise that you care about them with your positive and heartfelt friendliness.

Time on your own

Time is precious, but it is possible to work out a system to use your time optimally so that you can enjoy your life. Put aside just one hour a day, or one extra day a week for yourself ... time for you to do what your heart desires!

Happiness is a choice

Even in difficult times happiness is a choice that can turn your tragedies into victories. What a fabulous thought! You can choose to transform your problems, crises and hardship into happiness; thereby you will be changing them into victories.

Choose happiness!

You probably would have more time left to live a meaningful life if you started doing something for yourself for a change! Decide to stand still for a while and enjoy your life. Rid yourself of frustrations and worries. Choose to be happy and enjoy your life!

Sing a happy song

When you are happy, you can't help but sing. However, we have become so used to only seeing the dark side of life. Maybe it is time to start singing songs of joy again; a song of praise straight from your heart!

Life can be a delight!

Your attitude not only influences your personality, but also the quality of your life. Your life can be a disaster or a pleasure depending on the way you look at things. Only you can decide whether you want to go through life being depressed or joyful.

Keep book of your blessings

You have the power to make your life a pleasure, to count your blessings every day and to look at the bright side of life. If you start adding up your blessings, you will realise that your life is full of them. Don't allow these good fortunes to pass you by unnoticed. Cherish them, and be thankful!

Happiness warms your heart

If you keep your eyes on the warm rays of the Eternal Sun, your life will be complete and His healing rays will keep you warm. But if you look away, your joy will disappear in the darkness of your own shadow. Then you will only see the negative things ... your own fears and insecurities, and the hate and distress of the world!

Think positive!

Your mind has enormous power. The things you think about can make your life a success or a failure, or cause you to be happy or unhappy. Only you can decide what you think about ... Happy thoughts add brightness and colour to your life, while gloomy thoughts fill your life with misery and distress.

Be positive

People whose minds are filled with positive thoughts are happy, positive people. Fortunately, it's not too late for you to start thinking positive and being happy. From now on you should only have happy thoughts and choose to be a person filled with joy!

Happiness in gratitude

Gratitude and happiness make a good pair. Where the one is, you will usually find the other too. When you live with gratitude, the happiness wells up in your heart and spills over to your life. Just as you can teach yourself to think positive, you can teach yourself to live with gratitude ...